899 ✓

D0294926

WITHDRAWN

FROM STOCK

DDC(2) :

KURDS

Dr John King

Wayland

Titles in the series

Australian Aborigines
Bedouin
Inuit
Kalahari Bushmen
Kurds
Maori
Native Americans
Rainforest Amerindians
Saami of Lapland
Tibetans

This book has been produced in consultation with the Minority Rights Group; an international non-governmental organization working to secure justice for ethnic, linguistic, religious and social minorities worldwide who are suffering discrimination.

Series editor: Paul Mason
Designer: Kudos Editorial and Design Services

Picture acknowledgements
The artwork on page 5 was supplied by Peter Bull.
The publishers gratefully acknowledge the permission of the following to use their pictures: Rex Features 4 (David Grahame Baker), 6, 7 (Ozturk), 8 (Jacques Witt), 9 (G Sipalinogh), 11, 12 (Sipa Press), 13 (A Cavalli), 14, 16 (Sipa Press), 18, 25, 26, 27 (J Schneider), 28 (J R Wilton), 29 (Sipa Press), 30 (Sipa Press), 31 (A Cavalli), 32 (Aiza), 34, 33 (O'Donnell), 35, 37 (Sipa Press), 38 (Sipa Press), 40 (Kaveh Golestan), 43 (Sipa Press), 44 (T Hall), 45 (A Cavalli); Eye Ubiquitous 10 (J Burke), 19 (J Burke), 20, 21, 22, 23, 24, 36, 41 (JB), 42 (JB)

First published in 1993 by
Wayland (Publishers) Ltd
61 Western Rd, Hove
East Sussex BN3 1JD, England

© Copyright 1993 Wayland (Publishers) Limited

British Library Cataloguing in Publication Data
King, John
    Kurds.- (Threatened Cultures Series)
    I. Title II. Series
    305.891

ISBN 0-7502-0768-X

Typeset by Malcolm Walker of Kudos Design
Printed and bound by Lego, Italy

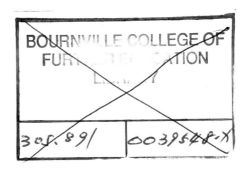

BOURNVILLE COLLEGE OF FURTHER EDUCATION LIBRARY

305.891   0039548-X

Contents

Introduction

▲ *An old Kurdish woman, part of a community in the mountains of Kurdistan. The Kurds have lived in the highlands that lie on the borders of Turkey, Iran and Iraq for many centuries.*

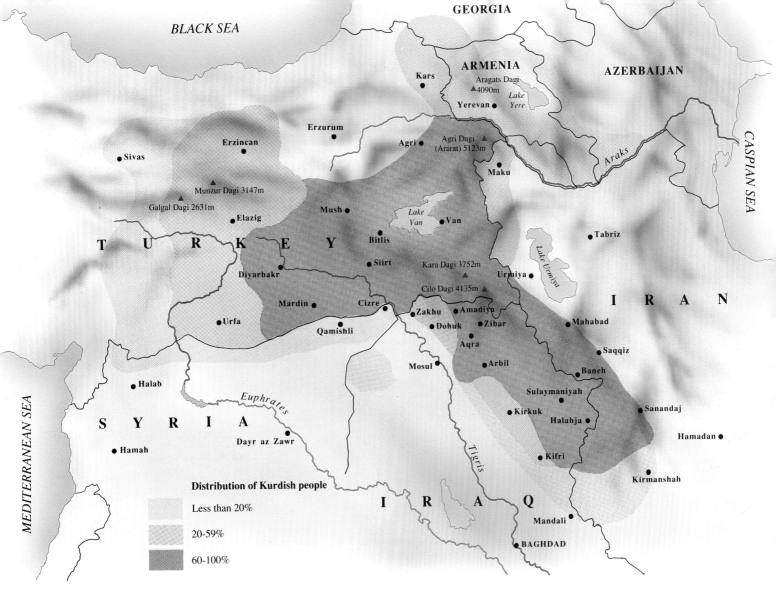

There are at least 22 million Kurds who live in the inaccessible mountainous heart of the Middle East, where the Iraqi, Iranian and Turkish borders meet. There are Kurds in these three countries, as well as in Syria, Lebanon, Armenia and Azerbaijan.

Emigration has also spread the Kurds all over the world. There are 400,000 Kurds in Germany, where many Kurdish men and women are now bringing up their children. There are Kurdish communities in other European countries. Kurdish exiles live in London and the Kurdish Institute in Paris promotes Kurdish culture. Kurdish communities live in the USA, in Canada, in Australia and elsewhere in the world.

The Kurds are unrelated to the Arabs, Turks and Iranians who live around them. Their language is related to Persian, the language spoken in Iran. They are distantly descended from Indo-European people who moved into the Middle East four thousand years ago. The Kurds then were fierce warriors, and Kurdish girls and boys were brought up to be proud of their traditions. Today they are still fiercely proud of their heritage.

The Kurds have their own culture and traditions, and they want their own country. Whether they are able to go on being Kurds, proudly speaking their own language and living their lives in their own way, may depend on whether or not they can get a country of their own. This is because the governments of the countries they live in want them to stop thinking of themselves as Kurds.

5

2 *A Kurdish boy in Iraq*

Ziyad lived with his mother and father in the north of Iraq. He called his country Kurdistan. He was born in the town of Arbil. His family had a little house just outside the town, built of brick, with an orchard and some fields. Ziyad helped his mother and father with their sheep and goats, and learned to read and write at the village school. He had an older brother called Massoud, and two little sisters named Hikmat and Nabila. In 1980, when Ziyad was still a baby, Iraq went to war with Iran. At first the war was far away in the south: the family saw pictures on television of the terrible battles and the Iranian prisoners of war. There were always pictures of President Saddam Hussein, the Iraqi leader, and the Iraqi generals. The television news said Iraq was winning the war. The television was in Arabic, which Ziyad and the other children learned at school, but they spoke Kurdish at home.

When the war moved closer, Iraqi soldiers came to the village. The Iraqis thought the Kurds were helping the Iranians. Many of the

▲ *Kurdish boys in their classroom. Although they are encouraged to think like young Iraqis, Iranians or Turks – instead of Kurds – most of them remain fiercely proud of their Kurdish identity and homeland.*

A Kurdish boy in Iraq:

'Over five thousand Kurdish people were killed at Halabja, and thousands were injured. My brother and I were saved from death because a few hours before the bombing we had gone out of town to a village for some reason. Then the Iraqi government started bombing the villages around Halabja with chemicals too. We had to go with thousands of other people towards the border with Iran. I walked with my grandmother and brother. Nobody took anything with them - we left all our things in Halabja. When we got to Iran they took us to a camp and gave us a tent. At the camp we found our mother and grandfather.' Asir Shawkat, aged 14.
(*Voices from Kurdistan*, Minority Rights Group, 1991)

The picture above shows the body of a mother and child killed in the Iraqi army's attack on Halabja.

Kurdish men were arrested by the Iraqi police and were taken away. Then there was a rumour that the Iraqis were taking the people from whole villages and making them get into lorries to take them away to the south.

Then, in March 1988, the Kurds of Arbil heard that the Iraqis had done something dreadful at the Kurdish town of Halabja, near the Iranian border. People coming from the east said everybody in the town had been killed with poison gas.

Ziyad's father explained to the children that all the Kurds had been struggling for a long time to have their own country, where they would decide on their own future. The Iraqis had always opposed them. He told Ziyad and Massoud that there were Kurdish fighters called *peshmerga* hiding up in the hills, who defied the Iraqis and were ready to die for the freedom of Kurdistan. Massoud said he wanted to join the *peshmerga*. Akram laughed and said Massoud could go when he was older, if they would have him.

In 1991 Iraq went to war again, and this time invaded the small, rich country of Kuwait, far to the south of Kurdistan. Massoud was eighteen years old by this time and had to join the Iraqi army. Ziyad's mother and father cried, but Massoud went off to the south in his Iraqi army uniform. It seemed strange when what Massoud really wanted to do was join the *peshmerga* and fight against the Iraqis.

Ziyad and his sisters never saw their brother again. Massoud went to Kuwait with the Iraqi army. But armies came from the USA and Europe, and Iraq's army was defeated and driven out of Kuwait. Massoud was killed when the Iraqi soldiers tried to escape through the desert.

Food was very scarce in the north, and there was no petrol for the lorries that brought things to the Kurdish villages. Most of the Iraqi soldiers were in the south for the war. So the *peshmerga* decided it was time to fight for Kurdistan. They came down from the mountains and drove out

7

the last of the Iraqi troops, and then they went into the towns and sent all the policemen and the Iraqi officials away.

For a few weeks the Kurds thought they were going to have their own country. They hoped that the Americans would help them against the Iraqi government. They tore down all the pictures of Saddam Hussein and put up pictures of their own leaders, Massoud Barzani and Jalal Talabani. But the Americans did not help them, and after a few weeks the Iraqi soldiers came

back. They had powerful guns and tanks, and the *peshmerga* were driven from the places they had captured only a few weeks before.

The people were very frightened of what the Iraqi soldiers might do: many Kurds went with the *peshmerga* up into the mountains by the Turkish border. Ziyad's family also went. At first they travelled in a lorry with some other families. Then they had to walk. It was very cold, and the little children got very tired. Eventually they camped at the top of a hillside. Some

▲ *The wreckage of Iraqi army trucks and tanks that tried to escape from Kuwait, following Iraq's unsuccessful attempt to invade Kuwait in 1991. In spite of the fact that the Iraqi government is bitterly hated by the Kurds, many of them were forced to join the Iraqi army and later died in the invasion of Kuwait.*

▲ *Kurdish guerrillas in a mountain stronghold. Guerrillas have been fighting in the hope of setting up an independent Kurdistan for many years.*

people were ill and died, especially the old people, babies and small children. People from European countries such as France and Britain came and gave the family tents and food, and foreign doctors came to try and help the people who were ill.

Because the Americans and British had not sent an army, just a few soldiers to help protect the Kurds, everyone was still very frightened of what the Iraqis might do. To save the Kurds from attack by the Iraqis, the Americans agreed to fly their planes from their bases in Turkey over the Kurdish lands.

Eventually Ziyad's father decided it was safe to go home, so they made their long way back to Arbil. The Iraqi soldiers had gone and were camped to the south: they were afraid of the foreign planes that flew overhead. The planes would attack the Iraqi soldiers if they came into the Kurdish country.

In 1992 the Kurds held an election to decide who should lead them. Ziyad was fourteen, almost a man, and he was very excited on election day, riding up and down with his friends in a truck covered in posters of Barzani, the Kurdish leader Ziyad's family supported. Everyone thought that the Kurds might now get their own country of Kurdistan at last. But the Kurds had been disappointed before.

Ziyad thought that if the Kurds still had to fight for their own country, he would go to the hills and fight for the *peshmerga* as Massoud had wanted to. His parents were very proud of him.

3 A Kurdish woman in Iran

In her village in Iran, near the town of Mahabad and not far from the frontier with Turkey, Shireen was about to be married. She was seventeen years old. She lived at home with her mother and two sisters. Her older sister Jahan was already married, and had a child, but she and her husband lived in the family home. Jahan's husband helped to support the family, because

Shireen and Jahan's father was away working in Mahabad. Their father sent money home, but Jahan's husband did the work on the farm.

Shireen's family kept sheep and goats, and farmed a plot of land. Their house was made of mud bricks, with doors and window frames painted blue. In the dusty courtyard were pumps to bring up water and old petrol cans to carry it

▲ Kurdish refugees who fled from the Iraqi army at the end of the Gulf War in 1991. Turkey allowed only a few refugees to cross its borders, but Iran gave many Iraqi Kurds shelter.

▲   *A Kurdish mother and her daughters shelter from the hot sun. Many Kurds in Iran live on small farms, growing food and using mules like the one in the background to travel around.*

into the house. In the winter it got very cold at night, and the family huddled near the bread oven that had got hot during the day.

Shireen was getting married to Jalaluddin, who worked in a shop mending television sets in Mahabad. That was where he had met Shireen's father, who brought him home to visit. Jalaluddin had his school leaving certificate and was well educated. He wanted to go to Tehran to work, or even abroad. Shireen had never been to school. Lessons were difficult because they were in Persian, which was different from the Kurdish the family spoke at home. And her mother needed her to help about the house.

The old men used to tell tales about how the Kurds had once had a country of their own with a government in Mahabad, for a very short time after the Second World War. But that was long ago, before Shireen was born, and after just a year the Shah had sent his army and stopped it. The Kurds were again governed from Tehran, the Iranian capital.

Shireen's father said that some of the people thought it might be better for the Kurds when the Shah was overthrown and driven out of Tehran in 1979. Soon, though, the Ayatollah Khomeini's troops put the Iranians in charge again. At least life was quiet.

A woman in Iran wearing a black chador, a cloth cover for her hair and clothes. The Kurds who live in Iran are not treated as badly as they are in Iraq, but they have to fit in with the ideas of the Muslim religious government. Among other things this means that women have to wear a chador, so the colourful skirts Kurdish women traditionally wear are rarely seen now.

There were still groups of men in hiding in the hills who wanted a separate Kurdistan in Iran, but most of the Kurdish people nearby just wanted to live peacefully. When Iran was fighting Iraq, Shireen used to hear the planes over-head sometimes, and there were terrible stories about what had happened to the Kurds across the border in Iraq.

In 1991, when the Kurds in Iraq were trying to get away from the Iraqi soldiers, thousands of refugees came across the border. Shireen wondered if some of them might be her cousins, and whether she and her family could do anything to help, but they didn't have much money and it was hard to know what to do.

Shireen was unsure what the future might bring. But she knew Jalaluddin was a good man and she hoped she would be happy. She was not certain how much she cared whether the Kurds had a separate country of their own, but she did not much like the Iranian soldiers. And of course

Shireen and her mother and sisters now had to wear a black *chador* (see picture) over their clothes when they went out into the town. When she was a little girl the Kurdish women didn't need to do that.

A young Kurdish girl

'*Pushing her small sister ahead of her, Zeynep prods at the geese to drive them back into the yard. She knows how to look after babies and has two younger sisters to attend to. Now she stands with her hands on her hips, imitating her mother, and bellows at Ozlem to walk in front of her and keep the geese under control. One day a man's family will come to see her father and will bargain with all the elders to fix her bride price, and then she will be decked with gold bracelets, earrings and necklaces, new dresses and new shoes, to fulfil her role as a Kurdish female in her community.*' (Sheri Laizer, *Into Kurdistan*, Zed Books, 1991)

4 A Kurdish man in Turkey

Mehmet was twenty, and lived in Kars, a town in eastern Turkey where many people were Kurdish. He was a taxi driver: he often waited by the bus station for people who came from other towns. He liked to talk to them, especially if they were Kurdish.

When Mehmet finished work he liked to go to one of the tea-houses near the bus station. Only men were out at night, and in the cafes they played games like backgammon and dominoes. In Mehmet's favourite tea-house you could hear Kurdish musicians play. Until recently, the singers were not allowed by the government to sing in Kurdish, but everybody knew that in spite of the Turkish language they were Kurdish singers and the songs were Kurdish.

When Mehmet finished paying for his taxi, he hoped that before he was too old he might

▲ *Men at a cafe in Turkey, passing the time with games and coffee. Kurds sometimes go to cafes to hear tapes of Kurdish singers.*

have enough money to get married. He had a cousin who lived in Germany and worked in a factory in Dusseldorf. Mehmet wondered if he should go to Europe to try to earn his fortune. Some people made enough money in Germany to come home and buy a farm. Then their relatives could live in comfort and work on the farm while they went back to Germany to work again.

▲ *Turkish troops in Kurdistan. Much of Turkish Kurdistan is under military government, which has caused resentment among even Kurds who do not support the PKK (a radical group campaigning for Kurdish independence that is banned by the Turkish government).*

Kurds in Turkey:

'There was dignity in the people I saw and filmed at their work – planting tobacco, shearing sheep, baking bread in tandoori ovens. And bizarrely, a timeless sense of peace filled the green valley; storks nesting on chimney stacks, women making jokes, and always children everywhere. If I stood for more than a minute, I would be surrounded by them. Crowded in front of the camera, jostling to get in shot, getting shooed away by the adults – they are like kids anywhere. Except that they will be unemployable when they grow up. One look at the birthplace written on your identity card, and that's it. No further education, forced rehousing, gratuitous arrest, torture – these things are so commonplace people don't think it remarkable. Families flee to the west and pine for the east.' ('The Kurds in Mus', Claire Allan, in *Kurdistan Report*, September 1992)

In south-eastern Turkey, where Mehmet originally came from, his family was poor. His father and uncle were dead. And there was trouble, because the men from the Kurdish Workers Party, the PKK, sometimes came in the dark and attacked the police and soldiers. Then the police were hard on all the Kurds. Boys Mehmet had known at school had gone to the mountains to join the PKK, and he didn't want them to come to any harm.

Mehmet understood what made the PKK angry. The Turks refused to let the Kurds speak their own language, except between themselves. They made the Kurds feel like second class people. The Turks had always been against letting the Kurds have their freedom, unless they agreed to abandon their own traditions and become Turkish in their ways like the rest of the population. And there was a tough military government in the south-east of Turkey where most Kurds live. The young people felt they had no future unless they could have an equal chance at life in a country of their own.

14

5 History and politics

The Kurds are descended from Indo-European tribes who four thousand years ago moved into the region they now call Kurdistan. The group of people called the Medes, who are mentioned in the Bible, are probably ancestors of the Kurds. The Kurds are also mentioned by an ancient Greek author, Xenophon, writing in around 400 BC, who says that a Greek army met some people called the Kardukhoi on the borders of Persia. Xenophon wrote that the Kurds of his day were very warlike, and defied the Persian emperor.

When the Arabs brought the Islamic religion to the region in the seventh century AD, the Kurds resisted the new religion and fought against the invading Arabs. But the Arabs won a great battle near the modern Iraqi city of Suleymaniyah in AD 643. The Kurds converted to Islam, but kept their political independence on the borders between the Arab, Persian and Byzantine empires for many centuries. There were Kurdish chieftains and rulers who made agreements with the neighbouring empires that meant they kept a lot of independence. But there was never really a unified state of Kurdistan, and the Kurds relied on the difficult mountain country and on the distance between them and the Arab, Turkish and Persian armies to keep them safe from their powerful neighbours.

During the Crusades the Kurds, whose fight-

Dates in Kurdish History:

1639 17 May   Treaty of Qasr-e-Chirin between Ottoman and Persian Empires, establishing their frontier in the Kurdish mountains.

1880 11 July   Sheikh Ubaidullah writes to British consul in eastern Turkey setting out the national claims of the Kurds for a Kurdistan of their own.

1908 23 July   'Young Turks' take power in Ottoman Empire, and recognize some of Kurdish rights.

1920 10 August   Treaty of Sévres (recognizes Kurdistan).

1923 24 July   Treaty of Lausanne (divides Kurdistan between Iraq and Turkey).

1926 5 March   Frontier treaty between Turkey and Iraq, giving the Kurdish area north of Mosul to Baghdad.

1945 16 October   Iraq crushes Kurdish revolt.

1961 15 November   Beginning of Kurdish revolt in Iraq led by Mustafa Barzani.

1966 29 June   Iraqi government claims Mustafa Barzani has accepted a peace plan.

1970 11 March   Iraq offers Kurds autonomy, rejected as insufficient by the Kurds.

1974 23 September   Iraq claims total victory over Kurds.

1975 6 March   Iraq and Iran sign frontier agreement. Iran withdraws help for Iraqi Kurds.

1980 12 September   Turkish military coup followed by mass arrests of Kurds.

1980 22 September   Iran-Iraq war begins.

1984 15 August   First PKK attacks in Turkey.

1988 17 March   Iraqis massacre Kurds at Halabja.

1990 2 August   Iraq invades Kuwait.

1991 10 April   Air exclusion zone agreed by United Nations.

1991 13 April   US President Bush says he will not become involved in any civil war in Iraq.

1992 19 May   Kurdish parliament elected in northern Iraq.

ing men were fierce warriors, made their influence felt widely in the territory which is Syria, Lebanon and Israel today. The Muslim hero Saladin (Salah al-Din Yusuf), born in AD 1138, was a Kurd. Saladin fought against the crusaders and became King of Egypt (in 1169) and Syria (in 1186). Many of his soldiers were Kurds.

After a battle at Lake Van in 1514 between Persia and the armies of the Ottoman Empire

Kurds in Lebanon

There are perhaps 100,000 Kurds in Lebanon today, where they are not thought to be very important. Their identity cards do not give them full Lebanese citizenship, even if their families have lived in Lebanon for generations.

The difficult treatment the Kurds have had to endure in Lebanon made them sympathetic to the left-wing PKK. Lebanese Kurds, and Kurds from elsewhere in the world, attend the guerrilla training camp known as the Mahsum Korkmaz Academy. This was set up by the PKK in Lebanon's Bekaa Valley, an area of Lebanon controlled by Syria. In 1992 Turkey asked Syria to stop guerrilla training there. The PKK guerilla training in Lebanon may not continue if Turkey is successful in putting pressure on its Arab neighbours to bring it to an end.

▲   *Kurdish peshmerga guerrillas: the word peshmerga means one who faces death. Ever since the First World War, somewhere in Kurdistan there have been peshmerga fighters who are willing to die to free their country.*

most of the Kurds came under Ottoman rule, but kept much local independence. Other Kurds served as frontier guards for the Persians.

The Ottoman Empire was broken up at the end of the First World War, in 1918. Britain and France, who were among the victorious allies in that war, agreed in a treaty made in 1920 to set up an independent Kurdistan. This was to be in part of the territory of modern Turkey and Iraq. However, the new Turkish leader Kemal Ataturk persuaded Britain and France that they should let him found a Turkish state. The Kurds were disappointed, but at first Ataturk said it would be a state for the Turks and Kurds to share equally. The Kurds hoped Ataturk would give them a government of their own. But instead he incorporated Kurdistan into modern Turkey, ruled by Turks. The treaty that had been meant to set up Kurdistan was forgotten.

In 1923 the Treaty of Lausanne arranged the division of Kurdistan between the different modern states of the Middle East. Most of the Kurds found themselves living in Turkey: they are the ancestors of the 12 million Turkish Kurds of today. Another large group were in Iraq, which became fully independent in 1932. Other Kurds found themselves living in Iran, and yet others lived in Armenia and Azerbaijan, which were part of the Soviet Union until 1991.

The failure of the Kurds to get an independent state in 1920 led directly to the modern problems of the Kurds. The Kurds did not forget their desire for a country of their own, and this began to clash with the ideas of the states in which they were living. Iraq is intended to be a state for Arabs, in which the language and culture are Arabic. Turkey is a state for the Turks, where Turkish is spoken and Turkish ideas control what happens. Iran is an Islamic republic, where Kurdish culture has to come second to Islamic beliefs and traditions. It is hard for the Kurds to fit into these backgrounds.

The Kurds have not ceased to struggle against the governments of the countries in which they live. There were clashes between the Kurds and the governments in Iraq, Turkey and Iran in the years in between the two World Wars.

In more recent times, Iraq offered the Kurds an agreement on autonomy in 1974, but talks broke down and in a short and brutal war thousands of Kurds died. In Iran clashes between Kurds and the Iranian army led to the killing of thousands of Kurds from 1980 to 1984. In Turkey there has never really been peace between the Kurds and the Turkish authorities.

The Kurds have never stopped fighting for an independent state, and in recent years they have come to believe that their culture will not survive if they do not achieve a separate political status. The threat to the Kurds is that they may lose their distinctive culture and become simply Turks, Iraqis and Iranians.

Kurdish Nationalist Movements

Iraq:
1) within the Iraqi Kurdistan Front:
KDP (Kurdish Democratic Party), founded by Mustafa Barzani in 1946. Current leader Massoud Barzani.
PUK (Patriotic Union of Kurdistan), split from KDP in 1975. Leader Jalal Talabani.
United Party of Kurdistan formed by merger of small Kurdish groups in 1992. Leaders Mahmoud Othman and Sami Abdul-Rahman.
2) outside the Iraqi Kurdistan Front.
Kurdistan Islamic Party
PAK (Kurdish Freedom Party).

Iran:
PDKI (Kurdish Democratic Party of Iran) founded 1945.
Komala (a pro-communist front) Founded early 1940s.

Turkey:
PKK (Turkish Workers Party) founded 1974. Leader Abdallah Ocalan.
ERNK Civilian wing of PKK.
ARGK Military wing of PKK.

 # Who are the Kurds?

◀ *A family in Turkish Kurdistan at a farm near Lake Van. Kurdish families are often large, because the people know their children will support them when they are older. At one time the Turkish government refused to recognize the Kurds as a separate people and called them 'mountain Turks'.*

Most Kurds live in Turkey. There are almost twelve million Kurds in Turkey, out of a population approaching sixty million in the whole country. Then there are over five million in Iran, four million in Iraq, a million or more Kurds in Syria, half a million in Azerbaijan and Armenia, and more than half a million elsewhere, including about 100,000 in Lebanon.

The four million Kurds who live in Iraq have suffered badly at the hands of the country's ruler, Saddam Hussein. It is the Kurds of Iraq who are most often seen in Western television news programmes. In 1991, many of them fled their homes, into the snowy mountains up by the Turkish border. The world's sympathy was aroused by pictures of whole families living in freezing conditions in tents, or tiny children and old people carrying heavy loads.

The Turkish Kurds have suffered a long history of repression by the Turkish government. Kurds believe they are denied their rights as citizens, because they are not allowed to use their language, and because they believe the Turks hate them and discriminate against them. In Iran the Kurds are treated more fairly, but they have to put the demands of religion before their own Kurdish identity. This is because Iran has a religious government.

Whatever country they live in, all Kurds have a lot in common. All Kurds speak Kurdish, and every Kurd recognizes the language of another Kurdish speaker. There are very different ways of speaking the language, depending on which part of Kurdistan a person comes from. The main dialects of Kurdish are Kurmanji in the north and Sorani in the south. The Kurds are very aware of the separateness of their language, which owes nothing to their Turkish and Arab neighbours. Their common language, and the traditions, tribal stories and folk tales that go with it, are something every Kurd is proud of. Men and women can tell the stories their fathers and mothers passed down to them about the history of their tribes.

Another thing most Kurds have in common is their religion: most are Sunni Muslims. Many Kurds also belong to Sufi religious brotherhoods. That means they meet to chant and dance together to worship God, as well as saying their ordinary prayers. These brotherhoods are very important in the life of Kurdish villages.

Though most of the Kurds are Sunnis, about a fifth of them are Shi'ite Muslims, like the Iranians, including most of those who live in Iran. Others belong to various sects, like the million or so Alevis in Turkey and the smaller group of 100,000 Yezidis, an unusual religion which has taken features from different faiths. Many Yezidis live in Armenia and Azerbaijan. A few others belong to smaller Muslim sects. There are even a few Christians living among the Kurds, who speak Kurdish like their neighbours and are sometimes regarded as Kurds. But it is not religion that makes the Kurds different from their neighbours: most of the people around them are also Muslim.

What makes a Kurd regard himself or herself as a Kurd is mainly the language, and the feeling of a long, shared history of common experience, much of which has been experience of trouble and persecution. The Kurds believe they all spring from a common ancestry and are proud of themselves and the way they are able to live in their inhospitable but beautiful mountains. They are also very conscious of their shared traditions and their ancient warrior past.

Many ordinary Kurdish men and women would like to live quiet lives with their families.

◀ An armed Kurdish man in Zakho, in northern Iraq, with his daughter. Even when caring for their families Kurdish fighters in northern Iraq carry their weapons.

▲   *These Kurdish refugees in northern Iraq live in a damaged army truck. A whole way of life in the Kurdish villages has been destroyed, and the people must survive as best they can. Every drop of water has to be carried to the camp in plastic containers.*

But they are caught up in the changing politics of the regions where they live. Though many Kurds in Turkey, Iraq and Iran take little interest in politics, they cannot ignore the political changes around them.

In Iraq, the Kurds still face persecution from Saddam Hussein in spite of having their own parliament and something like a homeland of their own. No Kurdish family there can face the future without thinking about change. In Turkey, ordinary Kurds in the south-east of the country hear every day about the battles between the Kurdish militants of the PKK and the Turks, and every Kurd knows someone who has been killed. In Iran the Kurds face the harsh rules of the Islamic Republic, and some of them

wonder if the chance will ever come to have a separate country. So all Kurds, wherever they live, know that they are different from the rulers of the country their villages and towns are part of. And they are aware that across the borders are other people who feel the same, and who tell the same stories about their past.

The Kurds know that in the past the tribes used to wander from one part of their lands to another. They never had to submit to the Turks or the Persians. They still tell the old stories about Kurdish heroes, and about the Kurdish chiefs who at one time or another ruled part of Kurdistan. Some of the greatest figures of the Muslim world have been Kurdish, like Saladin (see page 15).

Kurdish life

HOW THE KURDS LIVE

Traditional Kurds mainly live off the land, but they farm in different ways. Some live in the high mountains, where they keep herds of goats and flocks of sheep. Others live in villages in the valleys or down on the plains where they are farmers. The men and women share the work in the farms and the fields, and the boys and girls help from a young age.

There are also Kurdish towns. In Turkey, Diyarbakir and Van are Kurdish towns, and Diyarbakir is almost like a capital city for the Kurds. In Iraq, the Kurds live in Arbil and Kirkuk as well as in other towns in the north. In Iran, Mahabad is the main Kurdish town.

The Kurds today dress in much the same way as their Turkish, Arab and Iranian neighbours. In Turkey the men wear mainly Western clothes. In Iraq they add woollen coats and waistcoats, chequered scarves wrapped round their heads like turbans, and sometimes baggy trousers. The women wear a Muslim style of dress, often also with baggy trousers, sometimes under layers of skirts, and they often choose bright colours. But some women dress more like women in the West. The women sometimes cover their heads in the Muslim way, especially in Iran, where the Islamic Republic prefers women to wear a *chador* (see page 12).

Traditionally, Kurdish women wear brightly-coloured dresses and scarves around their heads. Now, the Kurds wear their traditional style of clothing less and less: instead they wear the clothes of the country within whose borders they live. ▶

Clothes

'There are two kinds of traditional Kurdish clothes – one for men and one for women. The women's dresses are different colours and have beautiful patterns on. They are long. The men's clothes are made of nice material – they are trousers and a top and we have a long piece of material that we tie round our waist. Men also wear a hat. If we go to a Kurdish party we wear Kurdish clothes.' Hazan Shoresh, aged 11. (*Voices from Kurdistan*, Minority Rights Group, 1991)

A Kurdish man wearing traditional baggy trousers herds his sheep. Sheep herding is one of the only forms of farming possible in the high mountains of Kurdistan, and is one of the most important jobs there. ▶

There is a traditional style of dress that is gradually dying out, where the men wear baggy trousers and waistcoats and the women wear their brightly-coloured skirts. Some Kurds still wear at least part of the traditional costume.

EMPLOYMENT

In the Kurdish villages of Iraq and Turkey, many villagers still work at farming and traditional crafts. But their apparently peaceful way of life has been increasingly disrupted in recent years by the effects of political clashes, especially with the Ba'athist government of Iraq, and with the government of Turkey.

The Kurds are herders, and goats and sheep are an important part of village life. The flocks and herds provide milk and meat, and sometimes products like leather and goat cheese can be sold. The women make things to sell, such as carpets, while the men look after the livestock. Flocks and herds are the chief livelihood of the mountain Kurds, some of whom are nomadic.

The Kurds grow fruit and vegetables to eat, and the villagers who live on the lower slopes or on the plains also grow wheat to make flour for bread. Some Kurds grow tobacco to sell, mainly in the local towns. In Turkey Kurdish farmers grow cotton which they sell. But most Kurds farm to feed themselves, not to make money.

The women make cloth and rugs, and some Kurdish men are expert at repairing the trucks they depend on to travel between villages and to the towns. A few villagers work as merchants, and others as blacksmiths or builders.

In villages on the lower slopes of the hills, and especially in the towns, the Kurds do many different kinds of work. They are shopkeepers, carpenters, plumbers, teachers and bank managers.

Because of their unsettled lives and their uncertain future, many young Kurds are looking to a future outside Kurdistan, and perhaps even abroad. In Iraq, it is difficult for the Kurds to leave their own areas, and it would be unpleasant for them to live outside the Kurdish region. In Turkey many young Kurdish men work in the towns. If they succeed there, they sometimes come home to find a Kurdish girl to marry, and then bring up a family away from Kurdistan. Few Kurds marry people who are not also Kurdish.

Some young men and women move abroad to work: there are as many as 400,000 Turkish Kurds in Germany. This is almost a quarter of

▲ *Kurds who live on the lower slopes of the mountains or on the plains often grow food to sell. Still other Kurds are traders in the towns, like these men selling wool in Van, Turkey.*

▲   *Kurdish children in school. They are normally taught in the language of the country in which they live, even though they are used to speaking Kurdish at home. This makes it hard for them to understand their lessons, and many leave school early and find it hard to get a good job later.*

the people with Turkish nationality who live in that country. There are also Kurds in the Netherlands and in other places in Europe. Some Kurds go abroad to get away from the police in Turkey, Iraq or Iran. Kurds who live away from Kurdistan often send money home to help their relations who have stayed behind.

LANGUAGE

In both Iraq and Turkey, the Kurds are encouraged to regard themselves as Iraqis or as Turks, and to abandon their separate Kurdish identity. In Turkey the use of the Kurdish language was forbidden until recently, and in Iraq it is not encouraged.

If Kurdish boys and girls go to school they normally have their lessons in Arabic or Turkish, even if the schoolteachers are Kurdish themselves. The radio and television broadcasts they hear and see are in Arabic, Turkish or Persian, depending which country they live in. Although this helps the Kurdish children to learn foreign languages it is not good that they never hear their own language spoken outside their homes. If no one around you speaks your language, you start to feel that it is useless.

Of course, having lessons in a foreign language makes it difficult for Kurdish children to get the best out of their schools. School work is sometimes difficult even when children can speak their own language. When they have to work in a different language it is even more difficult. Even when they can understand what is spoken, it is hard for them to write their homework and they often do badly in written examinations.

RELIGION AND POLITICS

The Kurds who live in the mountains often still regard themselves as members of different tribes. That means that they see themselves as related to other families who live near them, in a stronger tie than just being neighbours.

In the old days, a village or local leader known as the *agha* was often important in village life. The *aghas* still play a part, but their influence is not so strong now. Young Kurds in particular listen to the Kurdish politicians and the militant movements, and make up their own minds what to think and do rather than asking the older men as they might have in the past.

Sufi brotherhoods (see page 19) are popular

Social change

'Kurdish society itself has drastically changed over the past half century. One of the most significant changes is the movement of large numbers of Kurds away from Kurdistan, as migrant workers, displaced persons because of fighting, deportees or political refugees. Perhaps a quarter or a third of all Kurds live outside Kurdistan, and only a minority of them are ever likely to return. Until a decade ago, hardly anyone abroad, except for a few romantics, was interested in the Kurds. That has now changed. The Kurds and their plight have become known to European and American public opinion. Those who have left Kurdistan have perhaps contributed more to the strengthening of the Kurdish movement than they would have done had they been able to remain there.' ('Kurdish Society', Martin van Bruinessen, in *The Kurds*, edited by Philip Kreyenbroek and Stefan Sperl, 1992)

with the Kurds. The leaders of these brotherhoods (called *shaikhs*) often still have a good deal of influence over the other members of the brotherhood.

Today more people listen to the Kurdish political parties, the Patriotic Union of Kurdistan

◄ *There is not much work for the older men in Kurdish villages in Turkey. These two men pass the time in conversation. Their sons may have gone to the mountains, to fight for the PKK.*

Kurdish demonstrators in Berlin call for peace in Turkish Kurdistan. There are up to 400,000 Kurds in Germany: some have fled from the troubles at home, others have come simply to make money. ▶

and the Kurdish Democratic Party in Iraq, and in Turkey the revolutionary movement known as the PKK (Kurdish Workers Party).

The political difficulties the Kurds are facing mean that it is hard for them to keep their traditional way of life unchanged. Many Kurds in Iraq have had to move from their homes, both because of deportations enforced by the Iraqi government and because they fled from Iraqi troops after the Gulf War. In Turkey there is always conflict between the Kurds and the Turkish army and police. This has become worse since the PKK began its attacks on the security forces in 1984. The situation in Turkey is complicated by the rejection by some Kurds of the PKK's communist ideas: this does not necessarily mean that they do not want an independent Kurdistan. Other Kurds in Turkey have moved to different parts of the country and adapted to mainstream Turkish life.

8

Problems today – Iran

The first modern Kurdish nationalist was *Shaikh* Ubaidullah, who launched a revolt against the Shah of Persia (now Iran) in 1880. The *shaikh* tried to set up an independent Kurdish state, free of both Persia and the Ottoman Empire.

In 1919, another famous Kurdish *shaikh*, Mahmoud Berezendji, took control of the Suleymaniyah region of Iraq from the British troops who had moved into Iraq at the end of the First World War. *Shaikh* Berezendji, who called himself the King of Kurdistan, also had influence in Iran: in 1923 he fled there from the British.

During the Second World War Mustafa Barzani led another widespread nationalist uprising. Mustafa Barzani was the father of one of today's Kurdish leaders, Massoud Barzani. At the end of the Second World War, in 1946, the Kurds briefly had a state of their own in part of western Iran, with its capital at Mahabad. The Shah of Iran tolerated the new Kurdish state for less than a year, until he was able to send troops to crush the rebellion against him. Barzani fled north to the Soviet Union.

Since then there has been little effective agitation for independence on the Iranian side of the border. Both before and after the Islamic Revolution the Iranian authorities have kept the Kurds under close surveillance and control.

In the early 1980s the Iranian government thought of giving the Kurds some independence. But the plans did not go far enough for Kurdish leaders, and when the government troops were strong fighting began again. Some of the Iranian Kurds are Sunni Muslims like their cousins across the border in Iraq and Turkey. The religion of Iran is Shi'ite Islam, but the Iranian leader *Ayatollah* Khomeini said that as far as he was concerned there was no difference between Muslims who spoke different

◄ *General Mulla Mustafa Barzani, a Kurdish hero of the past. The picture was taken in 1946, when General Barzani became President of the Kurdish Republic of Mahabad, which lasted only a year. The little boy beside his knee, on the left of the picture, is Massoud Barzani, who is today head of the Kurdish Democratic Party and one of the main Kurdish leaders in northern Iraq.*

▲ *Iraqi soldiers at the front in the war between Iran and Iraq, which lasted from 1980 to 1988. The Kurds backed Iran in the war, and were attacked by Iraqi forces when Iraq feared the Iranian troops might invade Iraq in the north.*

languages. He meant that although Sunni and Shi'ite Muslims have some differing ideas about their religion, they are all still Muslims and therefore should be able to live together.

No Iranian government has ever wanted to lose any of its territory. There seems no chance that the Kurds could become independent from Iran with the agreement of the government. Tehran firmly crushed the Kurdish movement inside Iran itself in 1983.

The border between Iran and Iraq has always been a cause of conflict between the two countries. There have been constant border disputes: from 1980 to 1989 there was a bitter war between Iraq and Iran. The Iranian government has always offered limited help and encouragement to the Kurds in Iraq. This is mainly a way of annoying the Iraqi government. In 1991, after the Gulf War, the Kurds rose against Saddam Hussein. Soon after, many thousands of Kurds crossed the border to Iran because they feared

---

Modern Iran

'There is no difference between Muslims who speak different languages. It is very probable that such problems have been created by those who do not wish the Muslim communities to be united. They create the issues of nationalism, of pan-Iranianism, pan-Turkism, which are contrary to Islamic doctrines.'
(Ayatollah Khomeini, Iranian ruler)

▲ *Iranian peshmerga in 1980, members of the Democratic Party of Iranian Kurds (PDKI). The PDKI leader, Abderrahman Ghassemlou, was murdered in 1989 after talks with Iranian officials in Vienna.*

revenge attacks. The Iranian authorities opened the border and behaved generously to the Kurds, but probably only because they could later be used against Iran's enemy Iraq.

Iran's policy to the Kurds always has Iran's own interests in mind, and the government in Tehran would not allow the Kurds today to act against the Iranian state. The assassinations of Kurdish officials who were visiting Germany in September 1992 seem likely to have been the work of the Iranian secret service. The murdered men belonged to the Kurdish Democratic Party of Iran (KDPI), which was founded during the Mahabad Republic. This was not the first time Kurdish leaders had been killed in Europe. The KDPI's leader, Abderrahman Ghassemlou, was murdered after talks with Iranian officials in Vienna in 1989.

Kurds in Iran today have learned that the government insists they must regard themselves simply as citizens of the western part of the country. Though the government is prepared to recognize them as a religious minority and allow some of them to practise Sunni Islam, and though the use of their language is not forbidden, as it is in Turkey, they still have no separate status.

If a Kurd is prepared to regard himself or herself as an Iranian citizen, life in Iran is easier. Kurds occupy many government posts in the west of the country. But Tehran still appoints police chiefs and other key officials, and the Kurds feel as if they are living under supervision.

9

Problems today – Turkey

The struggle between Turkey's Kurds and the Turkish government goes back a long way. After Turkey was made an independent state under Kemal Ataturk in 1924, he banned the Kurdish language, clothes and all public activity by Kurds. He wanted to make the Kurds into Turks. Ataturk wanted a Turkish state, and he would not tolerate people who wanted to be different. The Turks even began to claim there were no such people as Kurds, only what they called 'mountain Turks'.

The Kurds rejected Ataturk's plan for them to become Turks, with their usual attitude of proud independence. There were terrible battles between the Kurdish people and the Turkish authorities in the east of Turkey in the 1920s and 1930s. Whole villages were destroyed, and people were moved away from their homes. Many thousands died in the fighting.

The Kurds were defeated, but never forgot their separate heritage. Over the years there has been quiet resistance by the Kurds, who in private have always used their own language and kept up their old customs.

Politically, the aim of all Turkish governments since Ataturk has been to make the Kurds forget their past and become Turks. That is, to make them a part of the nation, so that there would be no difference between Kurds and Turks. But the Kurds have never accepted this policy. The Kurds have long memories, and know that if Ataturk had kept his word, they would have a homeland of their own in southeast Turkey.

For a while after the Second World War, life was easier for the Kurds. There was a free election in 1950, and the Turkish Democratic Party won it. They allowed exiled Kurds to

◀ *Turkish Kurds. Even ordinary villagers in Turkey have become used to harsh treatment from the police and the army. There have been many reports of civilians being beaten, often without any obvious reason: this has led many young Kurds to support the PKK in its armed fight against Turkey.*

return home, and gave property back to those from whom the government had taken it away as a punishment. A new constitution in 1961 even allowed the Kurds to express their own ideas and have their own organizations, so long as they used the Turkish language.

But in 1967 the government of Suleiman Demirel again began to clamp down on the Kurds. (Suleiman Demirel was again prime minister of Turkey in 1992.) The government was determined to keep a close control of south-eastern Turkey, because it borders Iraq, Iran and the Soviet Union, and because oil resources were discovered there. The military regime that held power in 1980 clamped down on the Kurds yet more tightly, and the army ruled Turkey until 1983.

THE PKK

Because they were allowed less and less freedom to be Kurdish, the Kurds once again began to fight against the government. In Diyarbakir in 1967, there were the biggest anti-government demonstrations since the 1930s. And an important development in the 1970s was that a Kurdish leader called Abdallah Ocalan formed the group known as the PKK, or Kurdish Workers Party. The PKK is organized as a political party, but it also has a tough military wing. Since 1984, PKK groups have attacked the Turkish army and police in Kurdistan. Not all Kurds approve of the PKK, because their attacks often bring trouble to the Kurdish villagers. They are ruthless, and sometimes kill other Kurds who do not support them. The Kurdish villagers are mostly against the Turkish government, but they often do not like the communist ideas of the PKK. This is because the PKK say that their government would control the economy and agriculture.

The PKK was an offshoot of a group formed by Kurds at Ankara University in 1974, which aimed to get recognition for Kurdish language and culture. The PKK was more radical, with a mixture of nationalist and Marxist ideas. It is led by Abdallah Ocalan, who is called Apo, which means uncle, by PKK members. PKK groups launched their first attacks on Turkish targets in 1984. They were allowed by the Syrian

Women in the PKK

'The party has always attached great importance to the struggle of women for freedom and spared no effort in this direction. This struggle of ours has resulted in the mass participation of women in the revolution, and in women actively taking their place in society. Women are involved both in the uprisings and in the guerrilla struggle. There are now more than a thousand women guerrillas, and the number is increasing daily.' Abdallah Ocalan, interviewed by *Kurdistan Report*, September 1992

Abdallah Ocalan, leader of the PKK, a radical group fighting for an independent Kurdistan. The picture was taken in 1991 at the PKK's guerrilla training camp in the Beka'a valley, in Lebanon. It is called the Mahsum Korkmaz Academy: it was named after a PKK member who died in a battle against Turkish security forces.

government to use bases in Syria, and set up a guerrilla training camp in Lebanon.

The PKK attacks police and army posts in Turkish Kurdistan. The group's first aim is to establish a Kurdish state in Turkey. Eventually it would like to see a bigger Kurdistan in territory taken from Turkey, Iraq, Iran and even Syria. The PKK demands help and support from Kurdish villagers inside Turkey. Villagers who object have been attacked and sometimes killed. In Turkish villages the police search ruthlessly to try to root out PKK militants, so they base themselves outside Turkey and slip over the borders to carry out their raids.

PKK Guerrillas

'At the camp known as the Mahsum Korkmaz Academy, [named after a PKK member who died in a battle in Turkey] I found hundreds of people in well-cut olive drab military fatigues, much more disciplined and military in aspect than any of the local militias. Hearing English spoken, I soon found myself talking with Milan, an olive-skinned teenager who had come from Australia, where her Kurdish parents had gone for work. Now she was a soldier in the war against Turkey. "I am trying to forget I ever knew English", she said. "All I care about now is Kurdistan."' ('Confrontation in Kurdistan', Christopher Hitchens, *National Geographic*, August 1992)

▲   *PKK guerrillas in their camp in the mountains of Kurdistan, preparing for an operation against the Turkish army. The Turkish government has banned all Kurdish political parties, so the PKK is the only group left for nationalist Kurds to support.*

The PKK is absolutely forbidden inside Turkey, but it has many supporters, especially among young Kurds. South-eastern Turkey is very poor, and many of the young people do not see any future for themselves within Turkey. They believe that their only chance for change is to break free from Turkish control. In the early 1990s, increasing numbers of ordinary Kurds in Turkey secretly began to support the PKK. Even moderate Kurds came to the view that the PKK was their only hope for the future. A moderate Kurdish leader, Mr Mehdi Zana, a former Mayor of Diyarbakir, said the PKK was the only national Kurdish movement in Turkey, and that the people should support it.

In 1991 the Turkish government seemed to be trying to compromise with the Kurds. They made an important announcement that the Kurdish language would no longer be banned. This did not go far enough for most Kurds, because though it was no longer a crime to speak Kurdish in public, there were still no Kurdish newspapers and no Kurdish radio or television.

But that has not meant that the Turkish government has been any less tough in its campaign against Kurdish militants. Turkish intelligence agents have attacked people they suspect of being militants. And there have been more casualties in clashes between government forces and PKK guerrillas. Four thousand people died as the result of violence in south-eastern Turkey in 1992. The largest ever number of deaths in a single incident occurred in a clash when 200 people died in September 1992.

Within Turkish Kurdistan, the Kurds are largely controlled by Turkish police officers and Turkish troops. Kurds vote for local representatives but these representatives form part of the Turkish political system, rather than the Kurdish one. Kurds only succeed in playing any part in political life in Turkey today if they set aside their own cultural identity.

The struggle between the Turkish security forces and the PKK has involved both Turkey's neighbouring Arab countries and the Kurdish movements across the frontiers. Syria had been allowing the PKK to operate from its territory. Now the Turks have asked Syria to stop them. And the PKK had a training camp in Lebanon, in territory controlled by Syria. The Turkish government has also asked for that to be closed.

Meanwhile the main Kurdish movements in Iraq have begun to try to prevent the PKK from crossing the frontier into Iraq. The Iraqi Kurds have their own struggle with the Iraqi government, and they do not want to antagonize the

A Kurd in Diyarbakir, the largest city in Turkish Kurdistan. He must read the news in Turkish, because it is against the law to print newspapers in the Kurdish language. ▶

Turkish government. In 1992, the Iraqi Kurds helped the Turkish army to drive the PKK out of northern Iraq to stop them attacking Turkish targets from across the border.

The Turkish government wants to be seen as modern and liberal. Turkey has asked to join the European Community and wants to appear as an orderly state ruled by the law. But at the same time it uses force to kill or capture PKK members and those who support Kurdish nationalism.

Many Kurds, just like most other people, want to live quietly and to be allowed to try to make their living as best they can. Even Kurds who are proud of their cultural heritage sometimes reject the methods of the PKK. But at the same time they resent the way the government does not recognize them as a separate people.

Some Kurds have moved to non-Kurdish parts of Turkey, to try to escape police persecution. They try to live like other Turks, at least in the eyes of their neighbours and the authorities. If enough Kurds act in this way the Kurdish way of life could disappear. Meanwhile other Kurds avoid persecution entirely by emigrating. Kurds go all over the world, but most to Europe. Germany is the most popular destination, with 400,000 Kurds.

◄ *These men are Iraqi peshmerga. Iraqi peshmerga clashed in 1992 with the Turkish Kurds of the PKK, who were using camps in northern Iraq to launch attacks across the border into Turkey. The Turkish government threatened to stop sending badly-needed aid to the Kurds of northern Iraq unless they helped fight the PKK.*

▲ *A patrol of Turkish troops takes PKK members prisoner. The Turks, who are wearing white snow uniforms, have been scouring the high mountains for Kurdish peshmergas trying to evade capture.*

Kurds in Turkey

'The young boy stood by his picturesque village on the edge of Lake Van and expressed the quiet Kurdish determination that seems sure to confound Turkey's new tendency towards a military solution to eight years of separatist insurgency. "I want a Kurdish state, a Kurdish flag, red, yellow and green," he said, as if repeating a basic creed. "I don't want the Turkish flag any more." Why? Was he not grateful for the neat Turkish health clinic standing on the edge of the village? The only explanation the boy had was the one that can be heard all over the south-east of Turkey: a Kurdish consciousness has been awakened, a fact that Turkey has refused to accept seriously after decades of denying the Kurdish identity.' ('The Kurdish nationalist genie', Hugh Pope, *Independent*, 6 October 1992)

It is hard to say that the Turkish government has modified its old policy of trying to assimilate the Kurds. On the other hand, it is equally hard to see if that policy can ever be fully achieved. The Kurdish population is so large and determined not to become part of the larger state that however hard Turkey tries, it may never be able to absorb the Kurds.

If the Kurds cannot get a state in their own part of Turkey, and Turkey will not abandon its repression of the Kurds, perhaps the best hope for the future is that Turkey may eventually come to accept the possibility of some kind of federal state. This would recognize the Kurdish identity of the south-western part of the country. Otherwise Kurdish culture seems to doomed to face difficulties in the face of continuing Turkish repression and persecution.

Problems today – Iraq

38

It is in Iraq that the Kurds have been persecuted by the government to the greatest extent. But it is also in Iraq that the Kurds have come closest to their aim of setting up a separate Kurdish state. There are four million Kurds in Iraq, almost a quarter of the country's population.

At the end of the Gulf War, in February 1991, Allied forces led by the USA drove Iraq's army from Kuwait. It seemed that getting rid of President Saddam Hussein was among America's war aims. Some of then-US President Bush's statements could have been understood this way. Militant groups among the Kurdish population of northern Iraq rose up against Saddam Hussein and his government in Baghdad.

The rebels saw that the Iraqi state was in a weakened condition at the end of the Gulf War. They thought they would be able to overthrow Iraq's authority in the northern Kurdish part of the country and set up their own state. They also believed that they would get some help from the victorious United States. In fact, the USA refused to provide Iraqi rebels with the help and support they hoped for.

The result of the failed Kurdish uprising in the north of Iraq was that much of the civilian population fled into the inaccessible mountains of northern and eastern Kurdistan. The refugees then attempted to cross the borders into Turkey and Iran. Iran admitted refugees, but television pictures of the Turkish border showed men, women and children living in appalling conditions in makeshift homes in the mountains, without enough food and medical care. The world's sympathy was aroused, but in the end little was done. Turkey would allow few Kurds across the border: relief agencies did their best

◄ *During the Kurdish uprising in Iraq which followed the end of the Gulf War, Kurdish guerrillas took the opportunity to use a portrait of the Iraqi leader President Saddam Hussein for shooting practice.*

Sirwar

'*The women's union in the city of Suleymaniya is housed in what was an Iraqi Ba'ath Party Office before the Kurdish uprising. Here Sirwar Rasheed, the headmistress at a girls' school in Suleymaniyah, explained the problems Kurdish women face today in the urban environment. In one room of the building women were running a sewing workshop making childrens' clothes to sell in the market. Like many others, Sirwar has not received her teaching salary for months. She continues to teach but has not been paid. Like their rural counterparts, many middle class Kurdish women like Sirwar are also struggling to make ends meet.*' (Julian Gearing, 'The Ones Left Behind', *The Middle East*, December 1992.)

to help the Kurds in their mountain camps.

Some Western troops were moved into Kurdistan to help protect the population. The initiative that helped the Kurds most was a US decision to seek United Nations backing for an air exclusion zone. This meant that Iraqi planes were forbidden to fly north of a specific line (the 36th parallel). The area north of the 36th parallel includes much of Iraqi Kurdistan. American planes based in Turkey patrolled the sky to make sure the rule was obeyed.

In the safety this protection gave, the Kurds organized elections in 1992 for a Kurdish government, even though Iraqi troops were waiting just beyond the southern border of the Kurdish region. The Kurds now have a parliament in northern Iraq, and they hope that their lands will become either a self-governing zone of Iraq, or in time an independent state, which of course they will call Kurdistan.

The two main Iraqi Kurdish organizations have most of the seats in the Kurdish parliament and most of the posts in the new Kurdish government. These two movements are the Kurdish Democratic Party led by Massoud Barzani, and

▲   *The smaller man in the red and white scarf at the centre of the picture is the Kurdish Democratic Party (KDP) leader, Massoud Barzani. He is pictured planning his strategy just after the end of the Gulf War, when the Kurdish uprising against Iraq began.*

the Patriotic Union of Kurdistan led by Jalal Talabani. They have held a meeting of other Iraqi opposition groups, and are organizing resistance to Saddam Hussein in other parts of the country.

The Kurdish uprising of 1991 was the last episode in a long history of confrontation between the Kurds and Iraqi governments, dating from the end of the Second World War. In 1970 the then-Iraqi President Bakr proposed a peace agreement which recognized the separateness of the Kurds and accepted the idea of a self-governing Kurdish region. This never really worked, and broke down completely in 1974, when fighting began again and there was a short but fierce battle between the Kurds and the Iraqi

army. In 1979, the Iraqi Kurds thought they might get some help from the new Islamic government in Iran. During the war between Iran and Iraq, Kurdish armed groups fought against Iraqi forces in the north of the country. Iraq responded with attacks on the Kurds.

Many Kurds were forced to move from their villages near the Iranian border, and young Kurds were conscripted into the armed forces and moved away to other parts of the country. Iraq also attacked civilians in Kurdish areas.

The upheavals had a terrible effect on the lives of many women. In the closing months of the war between Iraq and Iran, the Iraqi government split up families and destroyed villages, fearing that the Kurds would help Iran's army.

Merina

'Everywhere, it seems, there are groups of women struggling to bring up children on their own. Behind typical Kurdish smiles and laughter exist conditions of extreme hardship. Take the case of Merina, a woman living in the rubble of Baroshke village. Merina talked quietly of the loss of her husband and the terrifying exodus that took place at the end of the Gulf War. Merina fled with her children over the cold, muddy mountains to Turkey. She did not want to talk about her youngest daughter. The cold had killed her. She was just three years old.' (Julian Gearing, 'The Ones Left Behind', *The Middle East*, December 1992.)

Many men disappeared, and have never been seen again. More were killed in the attempt at an uprising against Iraq after the Gulf War. Women were left trying to bring up children on their own, sometimes in dreadful conditions. Families who have lost their homes live in tents or in temporary shelters, sometimes in freezing cold conditions, and depend on charity for food. Women are trying to help themselves and their children, but many have a hard life. Women are often harshly treated by the Iraqis, especially if their men have been killed, and many have to live with terrible memories of maltreatment and cruelty.

For many years the lives of the Kurds in northern Iraq have been conducted against a

▲ *These Kurdish women and their children are living in a makeshift camp, having fled their homes. Because so many of the men have gone away to fight or have been killed, the women have been left to care for the children and to earn a living on their own.*

▲ *Kurdish peshmergas in northern Iraq patrol for signs of an Iraqi attack. The picture was taken towards the end of the Kurdish uprising in Iraq in 1991: the Kurds there were still fearful of an attack in 1993.*

background of disturbance and political up-heaval. Most of the people want to live quietly, but have been constantly harassed by Iraqi government. Many people think their best chance of a quiet life would be in an independent state or region of some kind. That is why the Kurdish nationalists are so popular in northern Iraq, and why Saddam Hussein is hated and feared.

In the same way that the Kurds in Turkey have been forced to act as if they were Turks, Kurds in Iraq have only really been able to take part in the life of the country if they regard themselves as Iraqi citizens and use the Arabic language. The ruling Ba'ath Party in Iraq is a purely Arab party.

Few Kurds have ever risen to a position of responsibility in Iraq. Few would want to. But many of them have been forced to serve in the Iraqi army. Young Kurdish soldiers were among the conscripts killed in Kuwait during the Gulf War.

Though the Kurdish language is not forbidden, education in Iraq is in Arabic, the government services work in Arabic, and the television and radio are in Arabic. The Kurds have always felt like strangers in Iraq, which has been run almost exclusively by the Arab part of the population. In a state of their own in northern Iraq, the Kurds could at last cease to feel like foreigners in their own land.

11 *The future*

Will the Kurds survive as a separate people? In the end, whether a people is distinct or just a part of a larger nation depends very much on their political status. This is particularly true of the Kurds. The Arabs, Turks and Iranians do not want Kurdish culture to be part of their countries, so Kurdish culture can only survive in another country. The survival of the Kurds as a separate people is therefore connected to Kurdistan, and the possibility that the Kurds might have a country of their own by that name.

Kurdistan is a name that has often been used in this book: for centuries it has been the name of the area where the Kurds live. But it is also the name that Kurds everywhere, wherever they are, call the independent state or country they one day hope to have. A state of Kurdistan need not be the whole of geographical Kurdistan. For the Kurds it will be a place where they can live and govern themselves, and where their own culture can survive.

An independent Kurdistan is what the Kurds have wanted for at least the last century. Long ago, the Kurds governed themselves, though they were not fully united. In past centuries, Kurdish chieftains and tribal leaders enjoyed independence in their inaccessible mountain strongholds.

But then the Kurds came under the domination of their neighbours, within the large empires that occupied the region through history. By the end of the First World War they had a clear idea of themselves as a separate people, with a national identity of their own, and

◄ *This Kurdish woman is ready to fight alongside her PKK colleagues for Kurdish freedom in Turkey. Kurdish women as well as men are trained at the PKK camp in Lebanon.*

▲   *This picture shows the extreme circumstances in which displaced Kurds in northern Iraq have had to live in the harsh winter weather in the mountains. But their spirit is hard to break, and the Kurds are as determined as ever to have political independence.*

legitimate demands for a country of their own. Even though the Kurds in the different parts of geographical Kurdistan differ in their outlook and experience, all Kurds feel a strong sense of solidarity.

What will become of the three young Kurds we read about at the beginning of this book? Ziyad, the boy in Iraq, may not have to go to fight the Iraqi army. Iraq's Kurds may get their own state, if the Western countries, especially the United States, do not forget them. Perhaps Ziyad will be able to grow up in peace. But he and the other young Kurds of his generation may have to put up with many more years of threats and harassment from Iraq.

Shireen, in western Iran, may be able to live with her husband Jalaluddin, in Mahabad. The Kurds are just one of many different kinds of people in Iran, and the government is not trying to make them exactly the same as other Iranians. But the Islamic government in Iran has strong religious ideas about how people should behave, and Shireen will have to fit in with these.

Mehmet will be able to drive his taxi in Kars, in western Turkey, and perhaps one day to have his own taxi business. But he will always know that the Turkish police are watching for signs of the Kurds organizing themselves. He will hear stories about raids made by the PKK on army posts or police stations. And he will go to Kurdish cafes to hear the songs by Kurdish singers that have had to be brought from abroad because they cannot be sold in Turkey. Or perhaps he will go to Germany, where he will lead a different life with different problems.

The Kurds have had many years to become used to living in a world where they have no country. Today, they fear that if they do not soon have a part of the world to call their own, their children and grandchildren will no longer be Kurdish, but will be assimilated into the countries where they live. A proud history and a fine tradition will have disappeared, and the young Kurds will have been forced to become Iraqis, Turks, or Iranians.

The Kurds are not the only people who have not got a country of their own. And some cultures have survived down the centuries without one. But it is tragic that the Kurds have suffered so much, and that for many of them the suffering seems destined to continue.

Kurdish nationalism

'Kurdish nationalism, a cause blithely overlooked by the international community for at least a century, is now being brought forcibly to the attention of the West. By its own actions, it is now obliged to take up the cause of the Kurds and reluctantly decide the fate of Iraq as a country. By giving the Kurdish resistance the impression that it had American backing for a renewed uprising, letting it down when it took action, and then intervening in response to worldwide horror at the fate of Kurdish refugees, President Bush raised the intractable question of how the United States would like to see the Middle East rearranged.' ('Kurds: what sort of new order?', in *The Middle East*, May 1991)

▲   *A Kurdish woman and her son look forward to an uncertain future: for the Kurds, much will depend on international help, as well as on luck and their own determination.*

Glossary

Agha An *agha* is a tribal leader (see entry for tribe).

Alevi The *Alevis* are a Muslim sect found among the Kurds, related to the Shi'ites.

Ataturk Kemal Ataturk was a Turkish nationalist born in 1881. He came to power when he founded the modern state of Turkey in 1921. He died in 1938.

Autonomy Autonomy is the right of a people to govern themselves, possibly within a larger political unit. Autonomy is usually seen as a step short of independence.

Backgammon A board game with dice and counters much played in the Middle East.

Bush, President President George Bush held power in the United States from 1988 to 1993. He lost power at the American presidential election of 1992, when President Clinton was elected.

Byzantine Empire A Christian state that made up the eastern half of the Roman Empire. Its capital was Byzantium, now Istanbul.

Chador A *chador* is the black veil worn over women's clothes in Iran.

Crusades Religious wars launched by the Christians of Europe against the Muslims in the twelfth and thirteenth centuries.

Exclusion zone A military exclusion zone is an area where hostile aircraft or ships are not allowed to go. The United States declared an air exclusion zone in Iraq north of the 36th parallel in 1991 to keep Iraqi aircraft from attacking the Kurds.

Gulf War The war between Iraq and an alliance led by the United States and Saudi Arabia, which was caused by the Iraqi invasion of Kuwait on 2 August 1990.

Iranian The people of Iran are called Iranians. This country was formerly known in the West as Persia, and its language is known in the West as Persian. In this book we have used the word Persian for the language and Iranian for the people of Iran.

Islam The religion of Muslims, founded by the prophet Muhammad, who lived from 570 to 632.

Marxist-Leninist Marx and Lenin are regarded as the inventors of communist doctrine. Marx was an economist and political philosopher. Lenin was a politician who put Marx's ideas into practice after the Russian Revolution. Communist ideas of political organization are often referred to by communists themselves as Marxist-Leninist.

Muslim See Islam

National identity A people's national identity means their consciousness of belonging to the same nation, which they think has a right to independence.

Nationalist A Nationalist is someone who feels a national identity (see entry).

Nomadic Nomadic people, or nomads, are people who regularly move with their livestock to better pastures.

Persian See Iranian.

Peshmerga A Kurdish guerrilla fighter. The word means 'one who faces death'.

Shah Before the Islamic Revolution in 1979 the Iranian leader was known as the Shah.

Shaikh A *shaikh* is a tribal or religious leader.

Shi'ites Shi'ites are Muslims who follow the faction who believed that Muhammad's son-in-law Ali should have been his successor. Over the years the Shi'ites have developed different religious ideas from Sunni Muslims. Shi'ites tend to rely more on the guidance of religious leaders than do Sunni Muslims.

Statehood Statehood is what a people are said to have when they have achieved a

government and a territory of their own.
Sunni Muslims   The majority of Muslims in the world are Sunnis, who believe that the leadership of the faith was correctly handed down after Muhammad's death, and have developed a body of religious law by which they believe Muslims should be guided.
Tribes   A Kurdish tribe is made up of a group of families who live together and regard themselves as related through descent from a common ancestor. Members of a tribe are generally loyal to each other.
Yezidi   A minority religion followed by a few Kurds, which includes elements from the ancient Zoroastrian religion as well as Islam.

Further reading

For younger readers
Voices from Kurdistan, Minority Rights Group, 1991.

For older readers
'Human Rights in Iraq', *Middle East Watch*, February 1990.
The Kurds: A Nation Denied, David McDowall, Minority Rights Group, 1992.
People without a Country, Gérard Challiand, Zed Books, 1980.
Historical
To Mesopotamia and Kurdistan in Disguise, EB Soane, 1912. (This will only be found in major libraries.)

Further information

MRG's Education Project produces learning material and information for teachers covering many aspects of minority rights. For more information contact:
Minority Rights Group
379 Brixton Road
London SW9 7DE

Survival International is a worldwide movement to support tribal peoples. It stands for their rights to decide their own future and helps them protect their land, environment and way of life.
 Membership of Young Survival costs very little. When you join you get a newsletter with a Young Survival pull-out page and the chance to buy T-shirts, games, tapes and other Survival goods.
Survival International
310 Edgware Road
London W2 1DY

Index

*Numbers in **bold** refer to pictures as well as text.*